D1249511

TOOLS FOR TEACHERS

- **ATOS:** 0.4
- **GRL:** C
- **WORD COUNT:** 27

- **CURRICULUM CONNECTIONS:** weather

Skills to Teach

- **HIGH-FREQUENCY WORDS:** fun, in, is, it, play, the, we
- **CONTENT WORDS:** cool, hot, outside, sand, sun, sunny, water
- **PUNCTUATION:** exclamation point, periods
- **WORD STUDY:** long /a/, spelled ay (play); long /e/, spelled y (sunny); /ow/, spelled ow (down); multisyllable word (outside)
- **TEXT TYPE:** explanation

Before Reading Activities

- Read the title and give a simple statement of the main idea.
- Have students "walk" though the book and talk about what they see in the pictures.
- Introduce new vocabulary by having students predict the first letter and locate the word in the text.
- Discuss any unfamiliar concepts that are in the text.

After Reading Activities

Ask children to think of reasons why we need the sun. Explain that it helps plants grow. Without it, the world would be too cold. It keeps us and everything on Earth warm. Fill two containers with water. Place one of the containers in the shade or out of sunlight. Place the other outside in the sun or near a window. After a few hours, have students touch the water in each. Which is warmer? Why do they think this is?

Tadpole Books are published by Jump!, 5357 Penn Avenue South, Minneapolis, MN 55419, www.jumplibrary.com

Copyright ©2019 Jump. International copyright reserved in all countries. No part of this book may be reproduced in any form without written permission from the publisher.

Editor: Jenna Trnka **Designer:** Anna Peterson

Photo Credits: Tom Morrison/Getty, cover (foreground); matthew25/Shutterstock, cover (background); wragg/iStock, 1; Skylines/Shutterstock, 2–3, 16bm; Fran Polito/Getty, 4–5, 16tm; skynesher/iStock, 6–7, 16tr; FamVeld/Shutterstock, 8–9, 16br; kali9/iStock, 10–11, 16bl; travnikovstudio/iStock, 12–13, 16tl; Sergey Novikov/Shutterstock, 14–15.

Library of Congress Cataloging-in-Publication Data
Names: Kenan, Tessa, author.
Title: Sunny / by Tessa Kenan.
Description: (Tadpole edition). | Minneapolis, MN : Jump!, Inc., (2018) | Series: Weather report | Includes index.
Identifiers: LCCN 2017061692 (print) | LCCN 2018008498 (ebook) | ISBN 9781641280082 (ebook) | ISBN 9781641280068 (hardcover : alk. paper) | ISBN 9781641280075 (pbk.)
Subjects: LCSH: Sunshine—Juvenile literature. | Weather—Juvenile literature. | Sun—Juvenile literature.
Classification: LCC QC911.2 (ebook) | LCC QC911.2 .K46 2018 (print) | DDC 551.5/271—dc23
LC record available at https://lccn.loc.gov/2017061692

SUNNY

by Tessa Kenan

TABLE OF CONTENTS

tadpole books

SUNNY

It is sunny.

It is hot.

We play outside.

water

We play in the water.

sand

We play in the sand.

We cool down.

The sun is fun!

WORDS TO KNOW

cool   hot   outside

sand   sunny   water

INDEX